I can draw
Dinosaurs

LONDON, NEW YORK, MUNICH,
MELBOURNE, AND DELHI

DESIGNED BY Karen Hood & Penny Lamprell
ILLUSTRATED BY Peter Chesterton
& the Peter Bull Art Studio
WRITTEN AND EDITED BY Carrie Love
PHOTOGRAPHY BY Andy Crawford

PUBLISHING MANAGERS Susan Leonard
& Joanne Connor
PRODUCTION Seyhan Esen
DTP DESIGNER Almudena Díaz
CONSULTANT Emma Drew

First published in Great Britain in 2006
by Dorling Kindersley Limited.
80 Strand, London WC2R ORL

A Penguin Company

4 6 8 10 9 7 5 3

ISBN-13 978-1-4053-1506-7
ISBN-10 1-4053-1506-7

Colour reproduction by ICON, United Kingdom
Printed and bound in China

Discover more at
www.dk.com

Contents

Useful stuff

ARTISTS USE ALL KINDS OF OBJECTS for ideas on what to draw. Get the effects of different textures with the materials below. Have fun looking for things to give you inspiration!

water soluble colour pencils

paintbrush

Colour in a drawing with water soluble colour pencils. Use a wet paintbrush to soften the colour.

colour pencils

rubber

pencil sharpener

charcoal

soft pencil

HB pencil

felt tip pens

oil pastels

Get drawing in your sketchbook... try out all the dinosaurs in this book

Sketchbooks
can be fun too!

Use colour paper to draw on.

Gather together
some cones,
feathers, and
shells to compare
their textures.

Cut out pictures from
magazines and newspapers to
help you with your drawings.

Look at plastic
dinosaur toys
to see different
shapes.

Dinosaur gallery

DINOSAURS ROAMED THE EARTH for over 150 million years. Bring them back to life with your pencils, pastels, and felt-tip pens.

Diplodocus

Triceratops

Euoplocephalus

Corythosaurus

Hypsilophodon

Lesothosaurus

6

Archaeopteryx

Compsognathus

Tyrannosaurus rex

Iguanodon

Stegosaurus

Tyrannosaurus rex

Styracosaurus

Velociraptor

Hypsilophodon

Head to head

THE NAME DINOSAUR MEANS "GREAT LIZARD". Each dinosaur had different features to help it survive. Meet dinosaurs of all shapes, colours, and sizes.

Troodon

Compsognathus

Edmontonia

8

Stegoceras

Compsognathus

Velociraptor

Suchomimus

Corythosaurus

Archaeopteryx

Iguanodon

Lesothosaurus

9

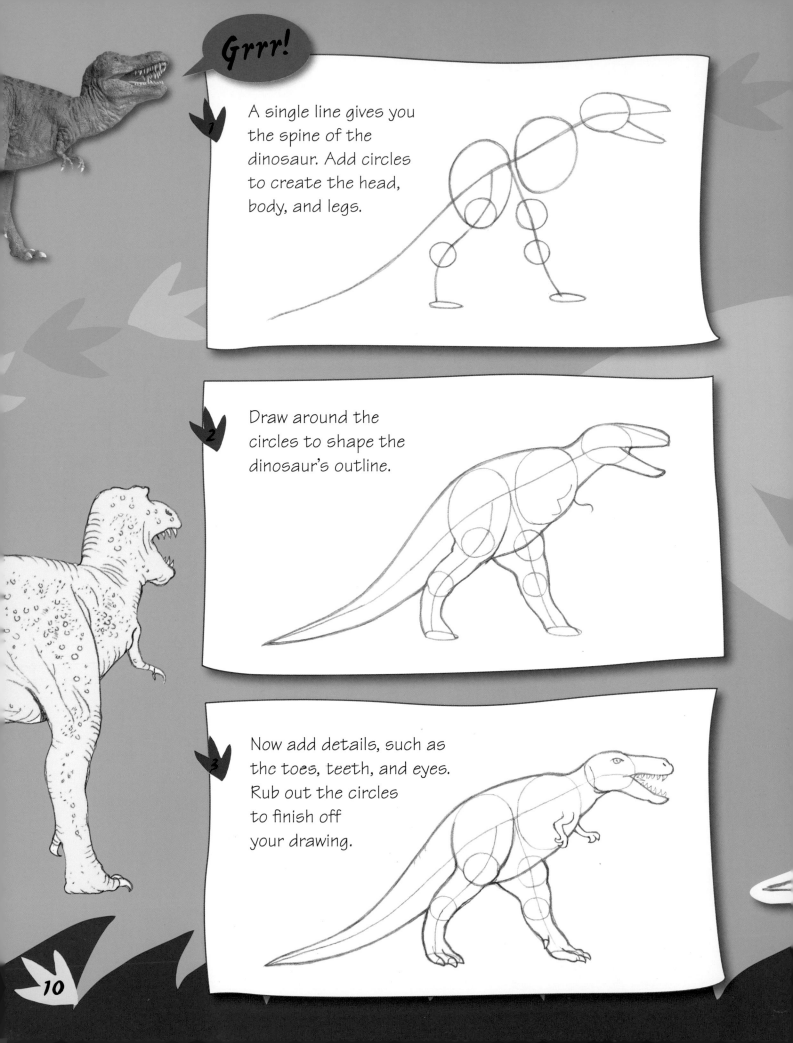

Grrr!

1 A single line gives you the spine of the dinosaur. Add circles to create the head, body, and legs.

2 Draw around the circles to shape the dinosaur's outline.

3 Now add details, such as the toes, teeth, and eyes. Rub out the circles to finish off your drawing.

10

T. rex

GRRRR! My name is T (Tyrannosaurus rex), one of the fiercest dinosaurs that ever stalked the Earth. I have big teeth as long as knives. Draw me at your peril!

1 Draw a curvy line for the main shape of the dinosaur. Add lines and circles for its head and legs.

2 Draw the body outline and give your dinosaur two more legs and an eye.

3 Continue to put more details onto your drawing until you get a finished picture. Use shading to give your dinosaur scaly skin.

Triceratops

MY NECK IS SHORT AND THICK to hold up my heavy head. You'd better behave or I'll come at you with my horns!

Grrrr!

First draw a line for the body shape. Use a small circle to create the head, and larger circles for the main parts of the body.

Draw an outline around the dinosaur to get the body shape.

Draw plates on the top of the dinosaur's back and add more details to its body.

Stegosaurus

I LIKE TO EAT PLANTS. My beak is sharp so I can bite off yummy green leaves. I protect myself from attackers with my sharp, spiky tail. See how well you can draw me!

Wow!

Textures

HAVE FUN BRINGING OUT DIFFERENT TEXTURES on your dinosaur drawings using pencils, pastels, and felt tip pens.

Triceratops

Recreate colours, shapes, and patterns on different dinosaurs' skin.

Corythosaurus

Stegosaurus

Compare the dinosaur on the right with the one on the left, and see how adding shading and texture has created a much more lifelike look.

Aaark! Give me some depth man.

Types of Textures

Draw thicker lines and stronger outlines with a soft pencil. Textures can make the dinosaur look 3-D.

Use charcoal or a soft pencil to show textures on a dinosaur's skin and bones.

To get the effect of scaly skin use a soft pencil for shading.

Words to get you going

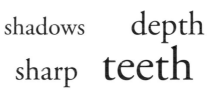

smooth feathers

shadows depth

sharp teeth

wrinkly skin

eyeballs shiny

scales lumpy deep

scratches

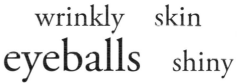

17

1. Use a line for the main length of the body. The tail will be as long as the neck and body.

2. Draw around the circles to get the shape of the dinosaur.

3. Give your dinosaur some claws and an eye. Rub out the circles and lines from step 1 to finish off your drawing.

Gallimimus

I HAVE A REALLY LONG NECK AND MY EYES ARE VERY BIG. I can swivel my head to see things in different directions. I feed on insects, plants, and lizards. Look how long my tail is!

Make the dinosaur's skin look scaly with shading.

Start with a long curvy line, smaller lines, and circles. The tail will look like the letter "S".

 Draw an outline around the shapes to make the dinosaur's body.

 Add a mouth and an eye.

 Give the dinosaur a nose. Rub out the circles and lines from step 1 to finish off your drawing.

I say!

Diplodocus

I HAVE THE LONGEST TAIL OF ALL THE DINOSAURS. My neck is made up of 15 bones – see how tall it makes me! My legs are as thick as tree trunks to support my weight.

Draw some trees and plants for me to live in.

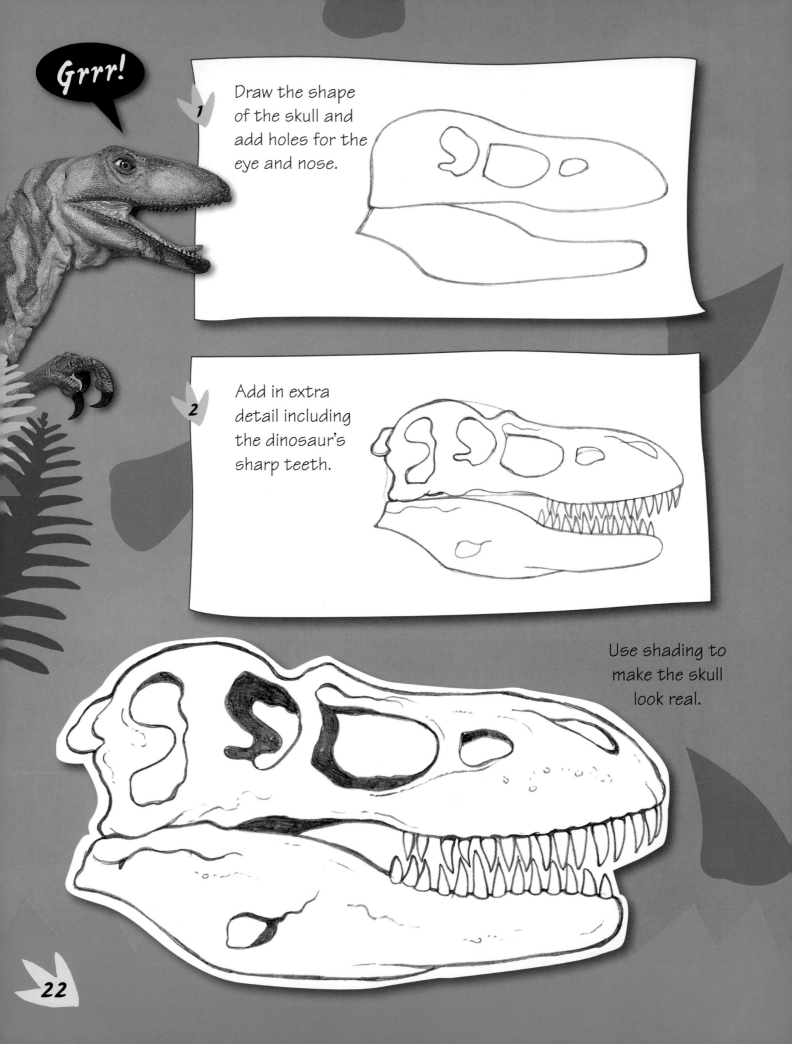

Grrr!

1 Draw the shape of the skull and add holes for the eye and nose.

2 Add in extra detail including the dinosaur's sharp teeth.

Use shading to make the skull look real.

22

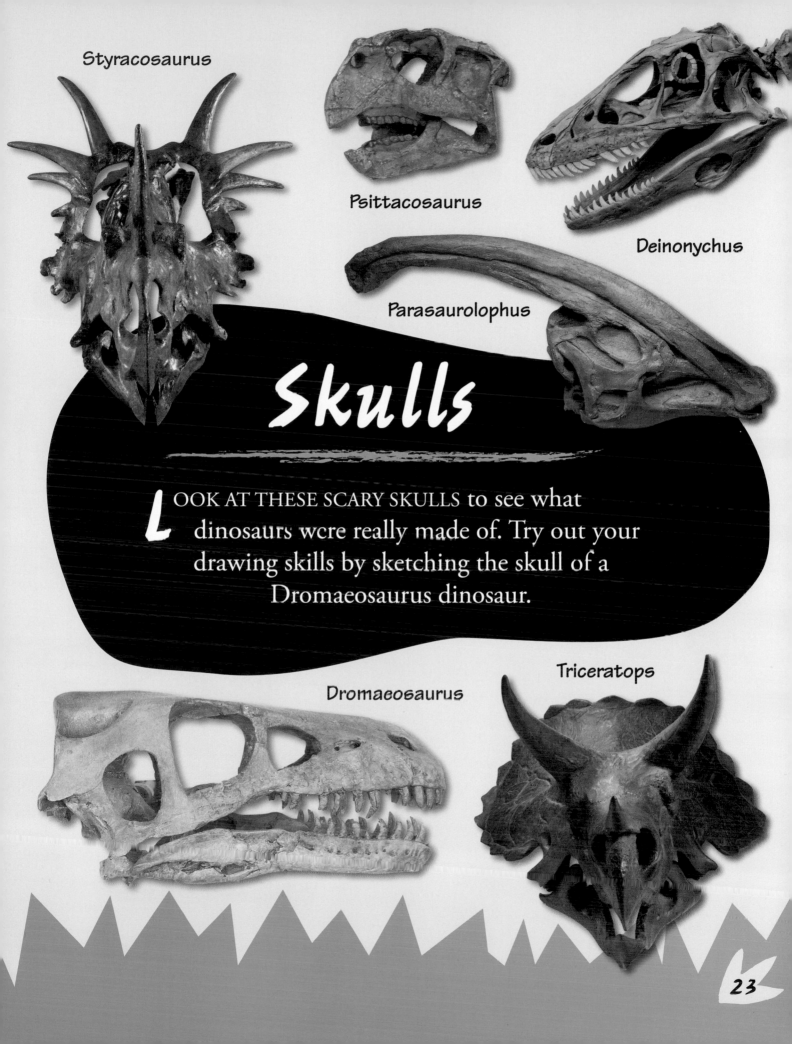

Styracosaurus

Psittacosaurus

Deinonychus

Parasaurolophus

Skulls

LOOK AT THESE SCARY SKULLS to see what dinosaurs were really made of. Try out your drawing skills by sketching the skull of a Dromaeosaurus dinosaur.

Triceratops

Dromaeosaurus

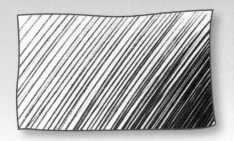

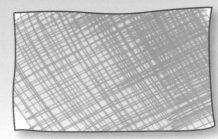

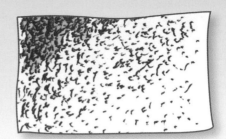

Soft, diagonal lines will add depth to your drawing, but make sure not to press too hard.

For cross hatching, make lots of straight lines close together, then add more going across them. Remember to press lightly.

Stippling means using lots of tiny dots to create shading.

I see!

Try out different pens and pencils to change the look of your dinosaur.

HB pencil, for general outline

2B, 3B, and 4B soft pencils, for shading

charcoal stick, for soft edges

pastel, for soft colour

felt-tip pen, for strong colour

rubber, for smudging

Compare the two images above to see what a big difference shading can make.

Shading

USE DIFFERENT TYPES OF SHADING to make your drawings look more exciting. Create a 3-D effect with thick lines, big and small dots, and colours.

I'm shady!

Use lots of colours to create a bright pattern on the dinosaur's skin.

Colouring in

HAVE FUN AND GET CREATIVE WHEN YOU COLOUR in your dinosaur drawings. See the difference that colouring pencils, felt tip pens, and pastels can make.

Try blending blues, greens, and yellows with your pastels.

Tyrannosaurus rex

Use light and dark coloured pencils to make the dinosaur's skin patterned.

Stegosaurus

Struthiomimus

Quick! The dinosaur is running away with the pencil.

Diplodocus

Larger dinosaurs would probably have had drab and dark colours on their skin.

Dromaeosaurus skull

Use yellow and cream felt tips for the bones and teeth.

I'm positively beaming!

Dinosaurs' skin blended into the background of leaves and trees. Use colouring pencils to make a dinosaur's skin green and yellow.

Triceratops

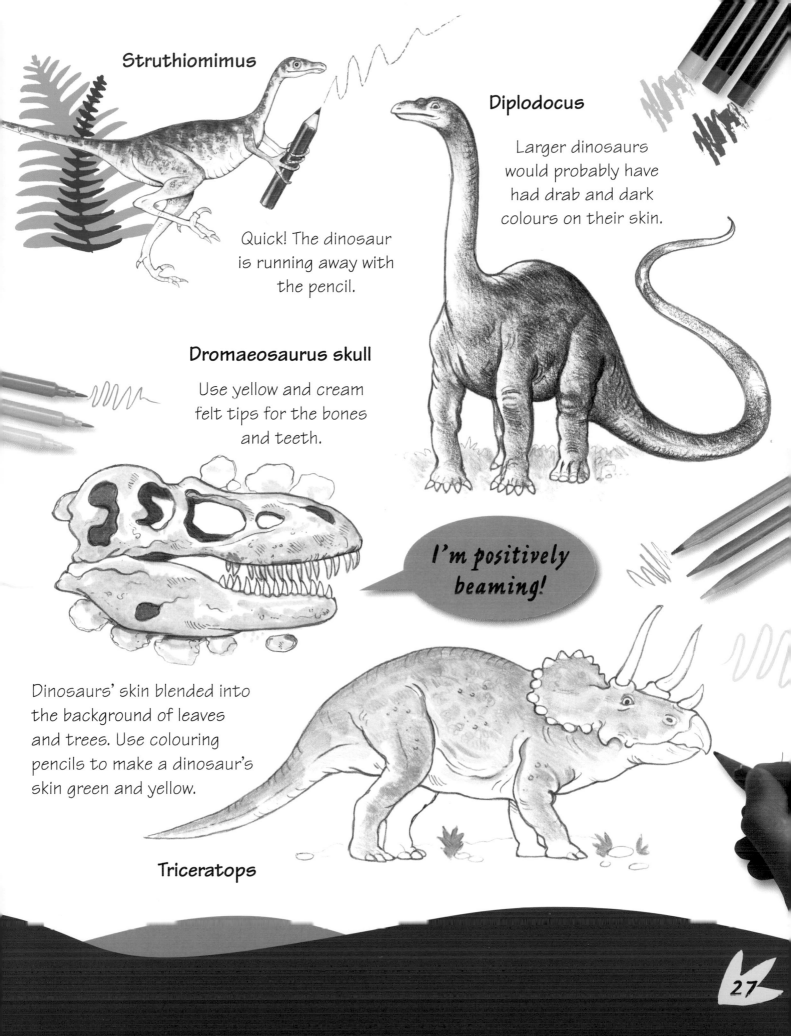

1 Begin with a long curvy line and lots of circle shapes.

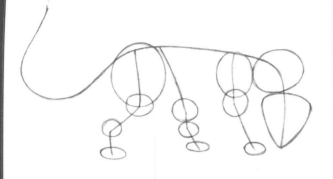

2 Draw an outline around the circle shapes for the dinosaur's body.

Euoplocephalus

I HAVE AN INBUILT CLUB AT THE END OF MY TAIL to scare away any enemies. I also have plates sticking out of my skin to protect me against predators. See if you can draw my armour!

3 Add horns, feet, and a tail.

4 Draw some plates on the dinosaur's back. Rub out the circles and lines from step 1.

1 Begin with basic shapes for the body and head. Use lines for the legs, arms, and tail.

2 Draw around the shapes for the outline of the dinosaur's body. The line will touch the circles.

Velociraptor

MY CLAWS ARE DEADLY. I use them to attack my prey. You don't want to mess with me so stay out of the way! See how well you can draw my claws and scaly skin.

Gnash!

3 Put detail on the dinosaur's arms and legs.

4 Draw eyes and teeth on your dinosaur. Rub out the circles and lines from step 1 to finish off your drawing.

Draw a pattern on the dinosaur's skin, and a bit of landscape for it to live in.

Draw some basic
shapes and lines to
begin your drawing.

Draw around the shapes
to create the wings,
head, and beak.

Finish off by adding details on the wings
and head. Rub out the circles and lines from
step 1 to finish off your drawing.

Pteranodon

I RULE THE SKIES. Although people often think I'm a dinosaur I am actually part of the reptile family. My wingspan can be up to 9 metres (30 feet). Get drawing my wings so I can fly up into the clouds!

1 Use a curvy line for the tail, and shapes for the main body.

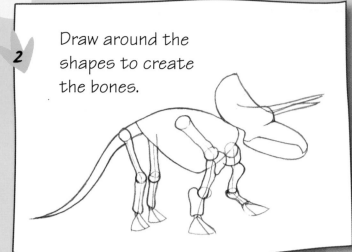

2 Draw around the shapes to create the bones.

Skeletons

SCIENTISTS LEARN ABOUT DINOSAURS by studying fossils that are dug up from the ground. Dinosaur bones have been found all around the world. Try drawing one!

Tuojiangosaurus

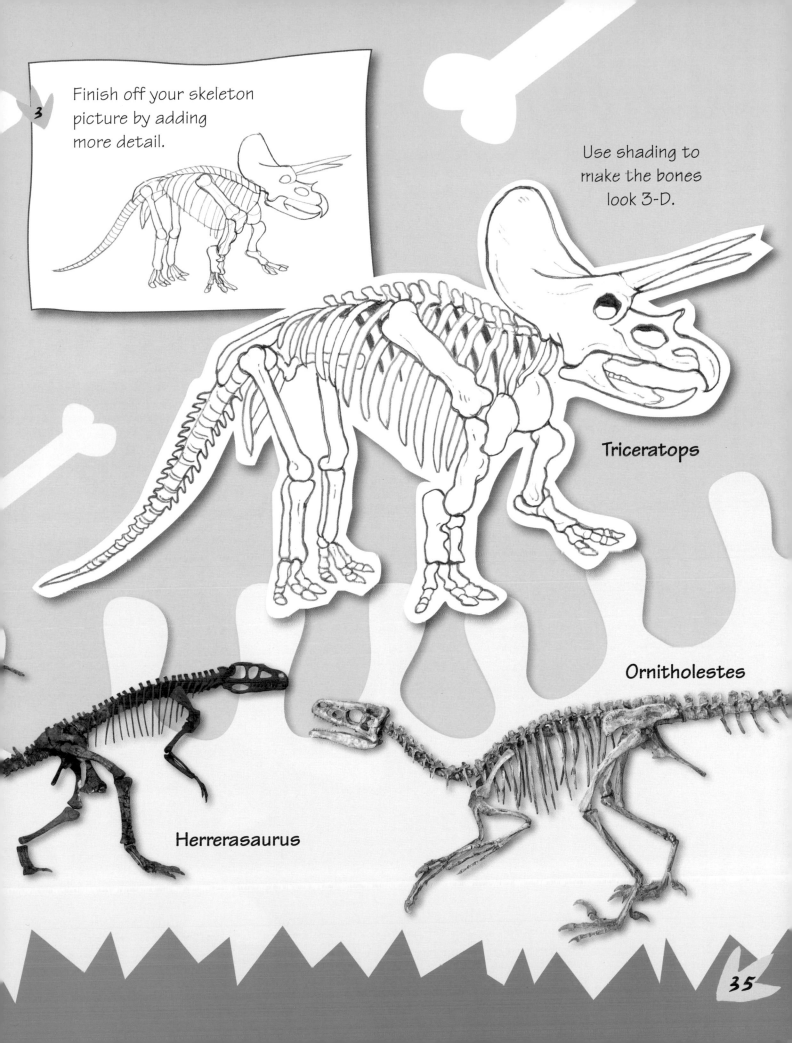

Finish off your skeleton picture by adding more detail.

3

Use shading to make the bones look 3-D.

Triceratops

Ornitholestes

Herrerasaurus

Colour

NOBODY KNOWS exactly what colours dinosaurs were. Scientists have made guesses by comparing dinosaurs to animals alive today. Patterns and colours on dinosaurs' skin would have helped them hide from enemies.

Red and orange will liven up your pictures of dinosaurs.

Use different shades of blue for feathers and some of the dinosaurs' skin.

Use green and yellow colouring pencils to brighten up your drawings.

Corythosaurus

Compsognathus

Giganotosaurus

Feathers

FEATHERS DECORATED SOME DINOSAURS as well as keeping them warm. See how well you can copy the textures and colours of the feathers below.

Fancy!

Velociraptor

Archaeopteryx

Look at my pretty feathers!

Archaeopteryx

Draw a squiggly line for the tail and body shape. Use small and large circles for the head, arms, and legs.

When you draw around the circles, the dinosaur begins to take shape.

Corythosaurus

I CAN MAKE SOUNDS THROUGH THE CREST ON MY HEAD. I have three toes on both of my feet, which are strong enough to hold up all of my weight.

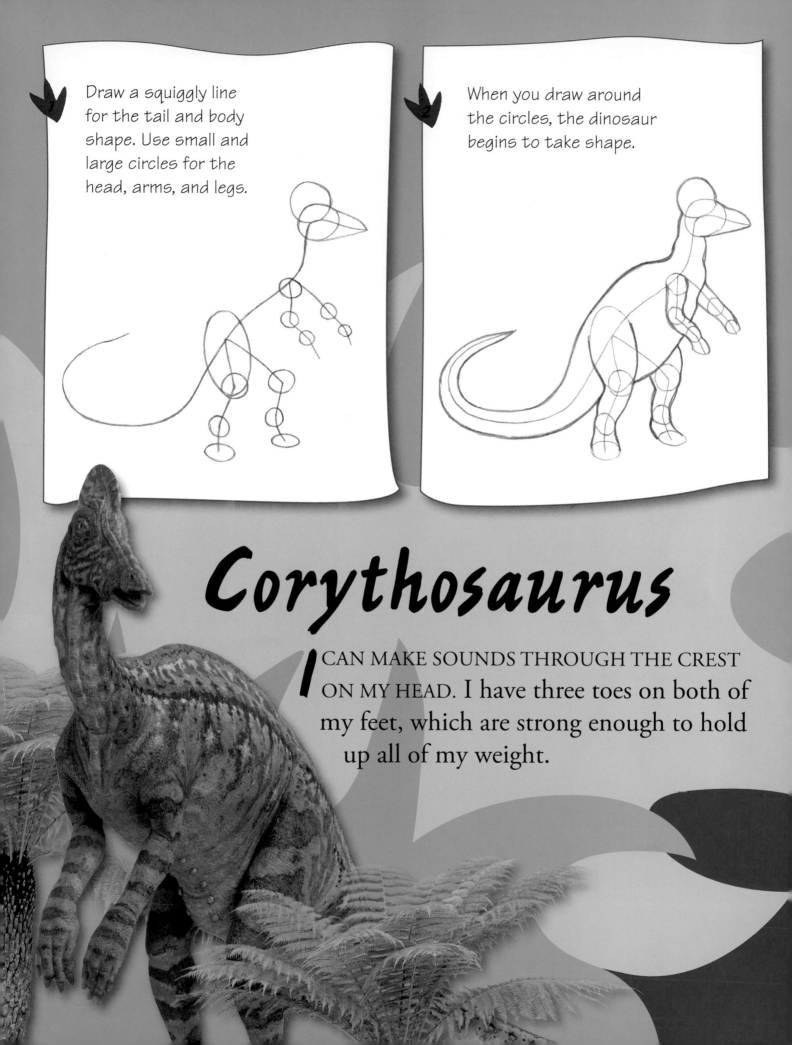

3 Give your dinosaur an eye and decorate the crest on its head with lines. Rub out the circles and lines from step 1 to finish off your drawing.

Using shading to make the dinosaur's skin look scaly.

Kerwee! Kerwoo!

1 Use a circle for the dinosaur's body and an oval for its head. Lines create its neck, tail, and flippers.

2 Draw an outline around the dinosaur's body and flippers. Add one eye.

Elasmosaurus
(Plesiosaur)

I RULE THE SEA, with my great long neck and tail. I swim around happily. I have large eyes so I can see my prey.

Complete your drawing by adding the dinosaur's teeth and nose. Use shading on its skin.

1 Use circles for the body, triangles for the hands, and a curvy line for the tail.

2 Draw an outline around the circles to make the dinosaur shape.

3 Add teeth, an eye, and claws to the dinosaur.

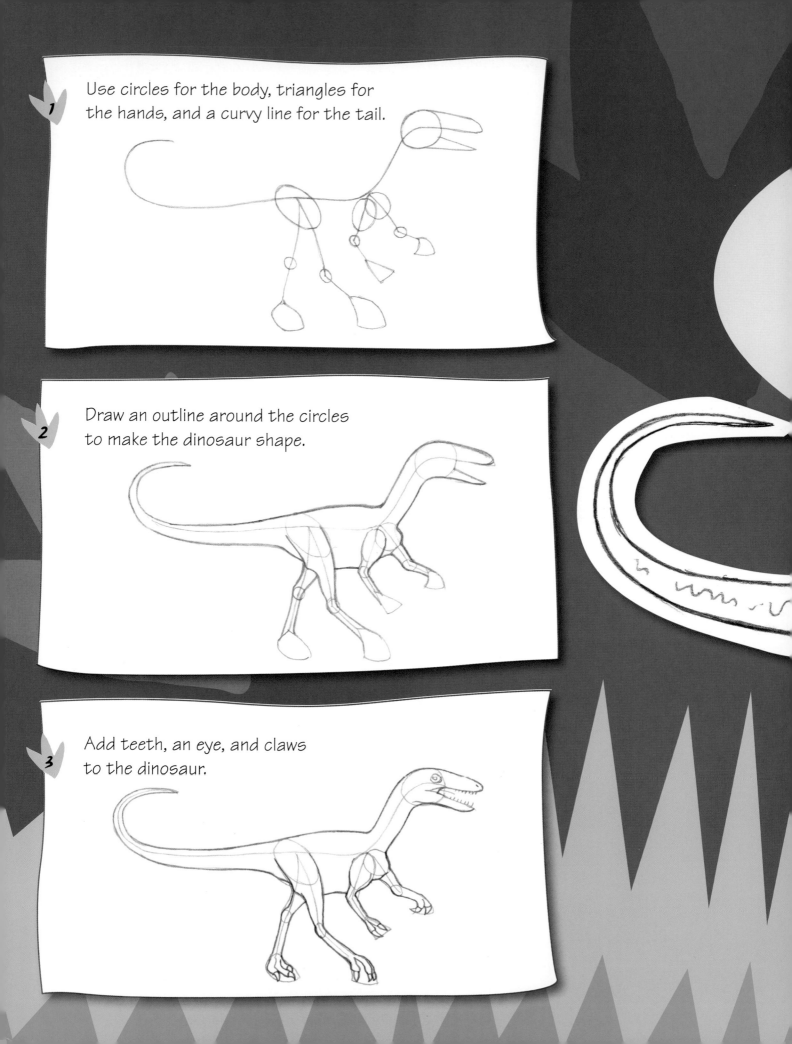

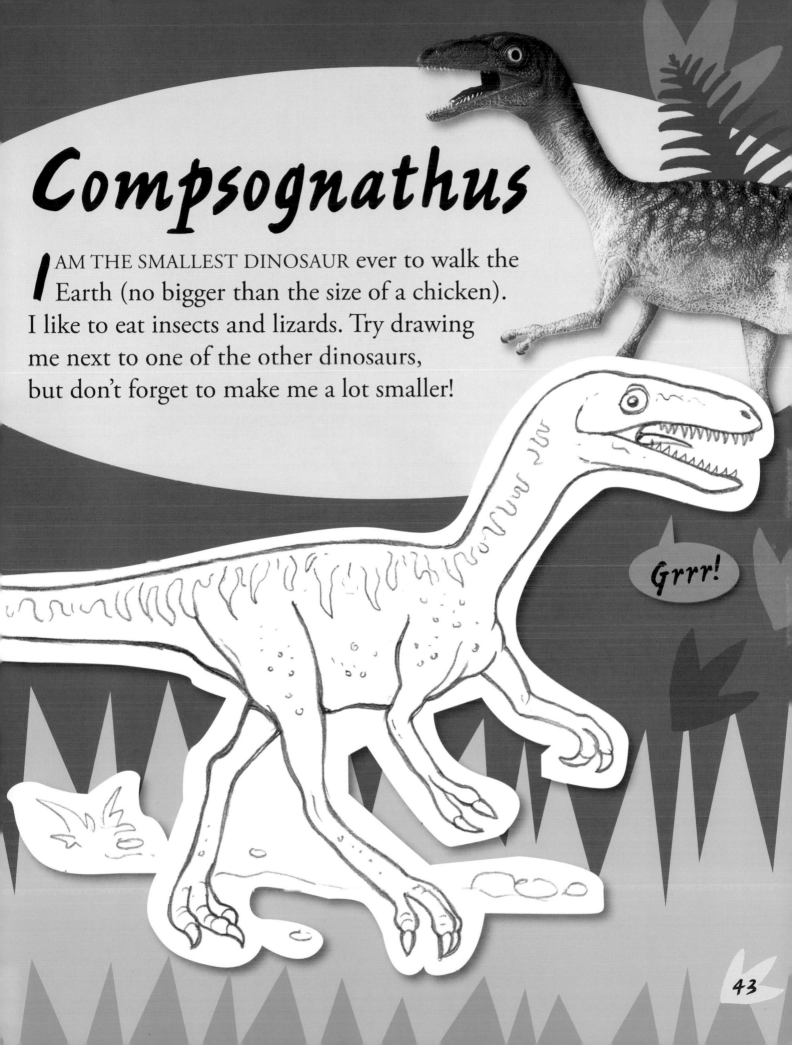

Compsognathus

I AM THE SMALLEST DINOSAUR ever to walk the Earth (no bigger than the size of a chicken). I like to eat insects and lizards. Try drawing me next to one of the other dinosaurs, but don't forget to make me a lot smaller!

Grrr!

43

Colouring in

When using pastels, smudge the colours together to get a soft effect.

BRING YOUR DINOSAURS TO LIFE by colouring them in. Add finishing touches like grass, plants, and the sky.

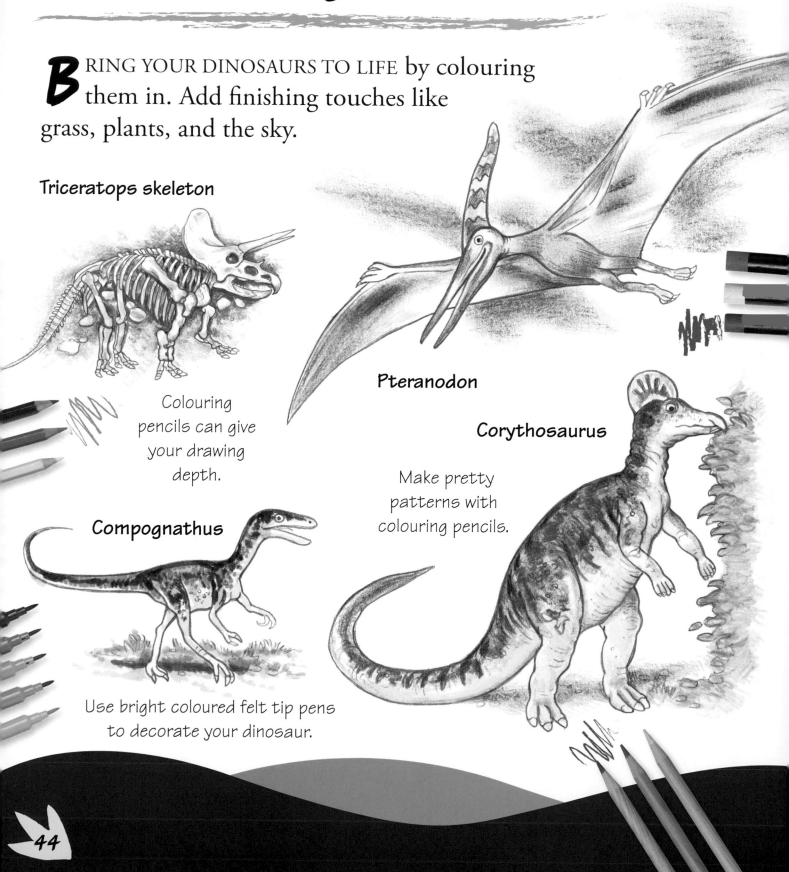

Triceratops skeleton

Colouring pencils can give your drawing depth.

Pteranodon

Corythosaurus

Make pretty patterns with colouring pencils.

Compognathus

Use bright coloured felt tip pens to decorate your dinosaur.

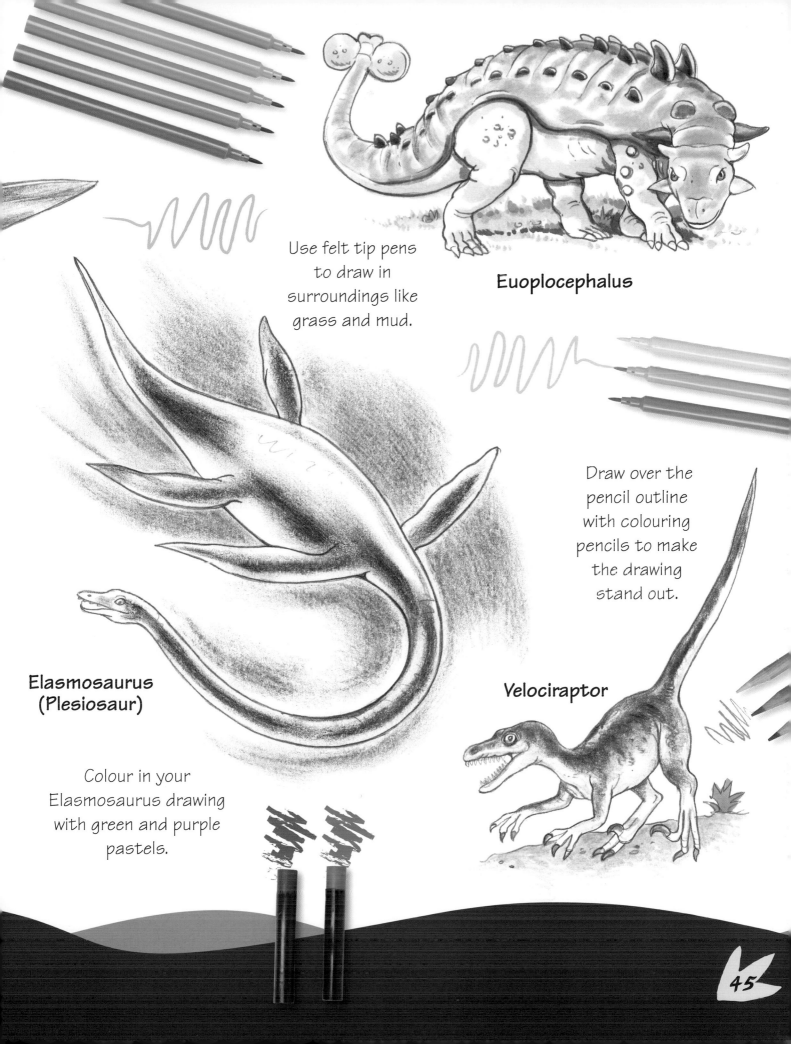

Use felt tip pens
to draw in
surroundings like
grass and mud.

Euoplocephalus

Draw over the
pencil outline
with colouring
pencils to make
the drawing
stand out.

**Elasmosaurus
(Plesiosaur)**

Velociraptor

Colour in your
Elasmosaurus drawing
with green and purple
pastels.

45

Scale

IF DINOSAURS WERE ALIVE TODAY some of them would tower above humans and buildings, although a lot of them would be smaller than an elephant!

Size and scale

See how big dinosaurs were when compared with humans. Look at how tall the Tyrannosaurus rex and Corythosaurus were!

Triceratops

Tyrannosaurus rex

Corythosaurus

Pteranodon

Velociraptor

Index

Bye! Bye!

Picture credits